Unhinged

The Poetic Justice of a Small Town Housewife

Peaches Voytko

BookLeaf Publishing

India | USA | UK

Made with ❤ on the BookLeaf Publishing Platform

www.bookleafpub.in

www.bookleafpub.com

Dedication

To Ford Joseph Voytko. Mommy and Daddy held onto hope because of you in our darkest hours. Heaven holds you, but you are in our hearts. Our bond is my safe haven, I know you would have had your Daddy's eyes. I miss having you with me everywhere I went. Thank you for making sure mommy was never really alone. Our hearts yearned for you dearly. Until we meet my sweet baby, by the Pen in my hand I swear you will live forever.

Preface

Thank you to everyone who takes time to read this. This collection was written over the last three years. While I want to leave my work up for your interpretation and reception, please know that there is always hope. Even in your darkest hour.

Acknowledgements

1. Trauma Bonds.

I'll forever get off on the euphoric highs and lows of wondering if you love me. Truly a personal mystery I live with. They'll frame our photo and tale a legacy of our lifetime in marital bliss. I'll smile from somewhere beyond this life knowing I painted a pretty picture. I credit myself the artist, the actress, the boring inadequate wife who was never interesting enough for you.

2. Unrequited Honesty.

How does one look a lover in the eye as they promise to change for you and tell them it isn't enough? My faith isn't where I wish it was. My heart has crept off my sleeve. You don't know me anymore, and I wonder if you ever will again. I gave you a chance when my heart was ready. You rejected me and time covered me with scars but failed to heal my wound. My heart forever stained by the depths of your ability to betray me, I find it hard to lay next to you at times. You sleep peacefully as I war with myself but I miss you before I can leave.

3. Blondes.

I want to paint you as the love of my life so badly, no matter how many times you cut my brushes and knock my canvas over.

I desire to be the reason that smile of yours meets your eyes. You look at me with such despise. I'm sorry I'm not her. More than you are, even. I want to make you happy. You play it cool but I know your truth. It will never be me for you. Reality never has felt fair enough, but the euphoric delusion of love has always been my favorite fix. We close our eyes as we kiss, a moment of temporary bliss. I know your discontentment will return when the lights come on. I wish so badly I could wake up as what you want.

4. Marital Bliss.

My marriage is Sanctimonious and holy, but it is hard. I hate the way he doesn't treat me but I love the way he does. I can't breathe here but I want to exhale worry and inhale trust so badly. I believe in magic for the sake of hope that he will grow but never change.

You see change is in far more than the seasons and therefore it scares me. Change is the leaves going from luscious lively green to autumns beautiful and brazen blush, it is also "I don't love you anymore" and "You're just a whore" but it hurts how it is easier for him than it is for me to walk out on us. How does one exist in both realms of blissful ecstasy and deep depression? The infinite answer is the taste of his delicious smile on my lips, and the sting of his inequities in my tears. I live in a state or confusion, on the clouds of love, but under the brewing storms of hate and resentment. We're both sorry, but he never says it first.

5. POV

I wish I could visit you from someone else's perspective.
To be someone who doesn't make you feel the things I
make you feel.
Someone you have a good relationship with.
Someone you really want. Someone who captivates your
attention without effort. It shouldn't be this hard for us.
Sometimes my marriage feels like it is simply a
fabrication of what I want.

6. Existential Comfort.

There's a me before you but I don't like to think about it. Comparison is the thief of joy.
I fantasize about exploding in a million liberating small pieces and out of existence every now and then. It's comforting. I live in a state of confusion. One last thunderous boom to stop the noise, I could never stop the noise. Regardless, part of me is forever trying to breathe, trying to understand and trying to trust that it works out in the end. Trying to trust that you want it too.

7. Lost.

I'm not sure which finds itself more agile, my heart or my brain. I get lost in my own expeditious resilience just to wake up with an elephant on my chest trying to decide if gasping for air is even worth it. When the Euphoria of making up with you wears off, I'm crushed by the reality that is unrequited love at times. I need to feel you in a way that you don't touch. I need to know you in a way that would require honesty. I understand why I don't ever feel safe in your arms but I'll never let go. Our world feels like it's made of sugar but will crumble if I'm not sweet despite the bitter it keeps serving me among all it has to offer. I beg you to love me, and you tell me you can't. It kills me, but a boringly familiar paradigm. It doesn't challenge me to grow beyond what I've always known. I hate the comfort of never truly expecting much. Of never believing. My words fall from my lips to the ground and neither of us care enough to pick them up.

8. Could Have, Should have.

I almost want to like him.
We spend so much time together.
We mutually agreed that we were just friends
who sometimes accidentally kiss each other.
I will not set myself up to fall and fail again.
We both have situations that make us off
limits to each other.
The things I feel make me want to shut him out,
as the wife of another man should.
But the way he holds me makes me feel okay.
He is a three AM,
Nike shorts and hoodie, text message invitation,
"Hey come over," King.
Sometimes he calls me babe, Holds me close when we
dance, Stares at me a little too long when he drinks more
than he needs, And tells me if he was looking for love, he
thinks it would look like me. I almost feel it, too.

9. Best Friend.

I almost want to like him.
We spend so much time together.
We mutually agreed that we were just friends
who sometimes accidentally kiss each other.
I will not set myself up to fall and fail again.
We both have situations that make us off
limits to each other.
The things I feel make me want to shut him out,
as the wife of another man should.
But the way he holds me makes me feel okay.
He is a three AM,
Nike shorts and hoodie, text message invitation,
"Hey come over," King.
Sometimes he calls me babe, Holds me close when we
dance, Stares at me a little too long when he drinks more
than he needs, And tells me if he was looking for love, he
thinks it would look like me. I almost feel it, too.

10. Timing is Everything.

I warned him not to play with fire, he said it keeps us warm. My intentions aren't to burn him, but my guarded heart keeps me torn. He has a sad soul. The kind you can kiss tenderly in the depths of the night, but well hidden behind a smile come daylight. He let me touch it once. He's dangerously attracted to me in a way I desire from home. I wish with the deepest passion we met at the beginning of eternity. I find myself anxious at the thought that someday, he and I will be reduced to ashes and secret
love letters. Time was never on our side.

11. Antimatter.

You are the cautionary tale of perfect timing. Ironically, it happened by a divine mistake. And for once in my life, getting it all wrong made it alright. It was nice to taste but my fear has always been wasted time. Haunted by the hands we held before, no one had a heart to spare. And leave our homes? Neither of us would dare. We can't linger here forever. I refuse to lie, if I have to it will hurt me to say goodbye.

12. I Will Miss You.

I once saw the day that we would have had the greatest love story of all times. Written to perfection, I'd read it in your eyes. We would dance on our porch, lit up by moonlight. My heart wasn't ready for the last chapter, the end. I type a goodbye text and reluctantly press send. Love isn't the solvent for all that we try to make it. Time is. Give yourself time.

13. Austin, TX

I almost moved to Austin last year.
I still wonder how a city like that would have held me. It
will forever haunt an insatiable curiosity thread into the
stitches of all that I am. Our fair secret is that it was you
who changed your mind.
The door you opened seemed to shut the more I reached
for it. I apologized for the mess I am to feel like I had
some control or say in the matter.
Like I hadn't changed too much to fit the landscape
designed so specifically for me. If cities were love letters,
I promise God wrote you to me. The idea of loving
another city that is afraid to love me back
wholeheartedly hurt too much to risk. Watching you
slowly slip through my hands felt like glass as our plans
fell apart.
But I am up late thinking of you again.it never stops.
Missing your wind in my hair, the way even rainstorms
fall beautifully for you. The way you make me laugh
until I cry cause I'm comfortable with you in a way I
don't think I deserve. This was always home and I didn't

recognize the feeling before I missed it. Forever a version of who I would have been. Of who I should have been. You were the light at the end of the tunnel from the beginning of time. You grew tired. I am a restless wanderer, still wandering impatiently while yearning for home.

14. Unfaithful.

I admit I liked being a villain better than a victim, but I hated hurting you. Every time he touched me you haunted my thoughts. I missed your hands. I felt so much but it was for you. He deserved more. Maybe I do too, but I have a strong preference of you.

15. Moment of Sobriety.

Toxicity sometimes comes crying in the middle of the
night, apologizing and telling you it loves you. You don't
deserve me,
But it'd be less than honest if I said I didn't wish you did.
You watched me cry, and the tears in my eyes did not
clarify the pain you were causing me. I offered a blind
man vision and you still chose to lose sight of your
blessing. That's all I wanted to be. My undying faith is
always willing even when my heart feels weak.

16. Internal Injustice.

As much as l want to hate you,
As much as I wish I could love him,
Our song will always bring me to my knees. It will
always take me back to the hope my heart overdosed on
to believe in you.
My personal demise remains a weakness for finding the
soft spot in hard hearted men.

17. Chasing the High of Trusting You.

It's a long ride down a dark road to reach the light of trust. It's almost as if you have to travel back through the broken pieces and try not to let them cut you as you attempt to find a way to breathe again. I remember sunnier days where I genuinely believed the sky was blue and the grass was green and you loved me. It didn't make my stomach turn the way it does on the days I remember, and I can't seem to forget. I didn't have the questions nor the answers I hold today. I didn't know the scent of resentment quite so well and now it's my personal odor.

But I want better for us. I want to be washed clean by new memories. I want my mind to be invaded so intensely by your love that I forget the things I hate about our past. I want to make love to you forever, and I never want you to leave my side. It's a lot to ask of myself, at times. But I can see the silver lining in your beautiful blue eyes. What lies ahead for our love is greater than the lies we left behinds.

18. She Wants a Baby.

My womb holds a place for a piece of you to dwell in me nine months long. The beautiful intimacy, the fruit of love making and the sacred connection it will bring us races through my mind every single day. In Gods perfect timing, and in my dreams, the resting desires of my heart granted. You and I forever live happily ever after.

19. Home.

I'd like to be the reason you toss your head back, laughing uncontrollably. I'd like to be the reason you realize that you're okay again, and that it doesn't hurt anymore. I'd like to be the "someday" that everyone promises you when your heart first breaks. I'd like to be the forever in your wildest day dreams. I want to fall again, I don't want it to be new. I'd like to fall in love again, with me and you. I know trust takes time and I have been distant, damn near gone. Sometime life leads us away, down the wrong path so we can appreciate home.

20. Conflicting Thoughts.

Our bond was inevitable. The theory of us begged the universe to press play. Your words were beautiful and decadent. You saw me when everyone else was blind. I wished on many stars for longevity in our journey but we never made it far before fear would steal you back.

Your eyes meet mine in a daze to remind me I'm too broken to be loved again. I'm a scarlet letter and timing will never align but it doesn't stop me from wishing it would. I'd love you forever, I'd show your fear that I could.

21. Redemption.

My head knows that there are probable consequences to the path my heart wants to take. My heart has made its peace with the potential pain of its own brokenness. It's made the choice, once again, dominating the wiser side of me. When the day comes to an end, and I'm laying in bed, contemplating what I want my life to be, I can only think of him. His tears are waves washing me far from the safety of the shore. I don't mind drowning because of them. His voice is the boom of thunder and the calm of rain simultaneously. He is the storm in which I center my peace, watching him destroy everything around me, but praying that he will never subside. I felt as though I looked into his eyes and simultaneously found the depths of the ocean and the very shade of blue that God reserved for the sky on perfect days. I felt the drip of cool rain after a long drought, the warmth of a womb, and the laughter of a child in his kiss. Our future in Marital Bliss.